And t

MW01135067

—

SUMMARY GUIDE

By EasyToDigest Reviews

Book Intro:

And the Mountains Echoed tells the stories of a

spectrum of characters whose lives intersect in

Afghanistan. The novel spans the last century, telling

how one man's choice reverberates through the

generations, affecting lives throughout the world.

Each chapter tells the story of a different character, and the love, courage, and heartbreak of each family.

Author Bio:

Khaled Hosseini was born in Kabul in 1965. His family was granted political asylum in the U.S. and moved to California in 1980. He has a medical degree from University California, San Diego, School of Medicine, and was a practicing doctor when he began writing. He is the author of *The Kite Runner* (2003) (adapted as a film in 2007 and as a graphic novel in 2011) and *A Thousand Splendid Suns* (2007). Hosseini visited Afghanistan as a Goodwill Envoy with the UNHCR in 2006, and afterwards established the Khaled Hosseini Foundation, a nonprofit that that provides humanitarian aid in Afghanistan. His

website can be found at www.khaledhosseini.com.

Chapter 1 - Chapter 1

Summary of chapter 1:

This chapter begins in fall 1952, late in the evening, with a father agreeing to tell his children a bedtime story. The father admonishes his daughter, Pari, and son, Abdullah, that there will be just one story, because they must get sleep before the father and Pari travel the next day. The father tells the fairy tale of Baba Ayub, a farmer who lived with his family in the small, drought-stricken town of Maidan Sabz.

While impoverished, the farmer's life was full of happiness with his wife and five children. One day, a *div*, a creature that terrorizes villages and steals children, arrives in Maidan Sabz. The *div* taps on

Baba Ayub's rooftop, which means he must choose one child to sacrifice to the *div*, otherwise the *div* will take all five of his children. Unwilling to choose, Baba Ayub writes the name of each child upon five rocks, and places the rocks in a sack.

He then grabs the rock of his favorite child, Qais, who is taken away. For years after, Baba Ayub is consumed by misery, until one day he decides to go to the *div'*s fort to seek revenge. After a long journey, the bedraggled Baba Ayub climbs the mountain of the *div*'s fort. The fearsome *div* offers to duel, but first shows Baba Ayub a beautiful garden, where Qais is playing with other children.

He tells Baba Ayub the children have good care and opportunity to live prosperous lives. He reveals that when he tapped Baba Ayub's house, it was a test to see if his love and courage was great enough to make such a choice to save the rest of his family. He offers Baba Ayub a second choice: to decide whether to return Qais to a live of poverty with Baba Ayub, or to let his son have this opportunity. Baba Ayub decides to give his son a chance for a better life, and the *div* provides a drink that removes all Baba Ayub's memory of his son.

Our storyteller tells Abdullah that the *div* offered mercy for once again passing a test of sacrifice for his son. Baba Ayub has a good life and is thankful for it, and no drought ever befalls Maidan Sabz again. And so the father concludes the story, and tells the son to sleep, since they will need to wake early the next day.

Character involvement: What each character is doing in this chapter.

The Father, the narrator for Chapter 1, gives in to his children and tells them a bedtime story.

Pari, his daughter, falls asleep before the end of the story.

Abdullah, his son, listens to the story and his father tells him to go to sleep when he has finished.

Within the story:

The *div*, a large mythical creature, offers difficult choices for a father to prove his love and courage.

Baba Ayub is tested by a *div* and proves his love of his family and his bravery.

Baba Ayub's youngest son, Qais, is taken by the *div*, and likely has a life of wealth and opportunity.

Lessons learnt in this chapter: What KEY points did we learn?

-The fairytale centers on the difficulties of making choices, and the rewards for a father who sacrifices for the sake of his family.

-The fairytale encourages satisfaction with a decent life, instead of wishing for more.

What emotions are raised in this chapter?:

- The love and affection a father has for his children – both in telling them a story, and in choosing one about a father and his love for his children.

- The frustration and despair for a father to choose to sacrifice his own feelings in order to gain a better life for his family.

- The anticipation of the trip that will start for the father and Pari the next day.

What questions are raised for the next chapter?:

Where are the father and sister going, and why?

What will we learn about this family?

Does this story of a father's love and sacrifice

foreshadow our narrator's story in the rest of the

novel?

Chapter 2 - Chapter 2

Summary of chapter 2:

This chapter describes the Father (Saboor)'s family and the incident that results in Pari being given to a wealthy family in Kabul. The chapter begins with Father striking Abdullah for continuing to follow Father and Pari rather than stay at home. Eventually, Father acknowledges that Abdullah will not give up, and allows Abdullah to travel with them. Father is pulling Pari in a wagon, and they travel for a full day, sleeping out in the desert, where Father refuses to tell them a bedtime story. While they travel, Abdullah walks in cheap plastic sandals because he traded his shoes for a peacock feather to add to Pari's feather collection.

Pari makes him promise that he will always live close to her. They reach Kabul the next day, and are blown away by the hustle and bustle of the city, as compared to their small village, Shadbagh. Uncle Nabi picks them up in a car, and takes them to his employer's grand house. Father is to build a guesthouse.

Abdullah is impressed with the running water, and compares the house and garden to the *div*'s palace. They meet Nabi's employers, the Wahdatis, and Mrs. Nila Wahdati takes the children to the bazaar. Abdullah cries when he realizes that Mrs. Wahdati will take Pari away from him. Mrs. Wahdati tells Abdullah that he will someday understand that it is for the best. That winter, Father cuts down the tree that held a tree swing for generations, in order to have firewood.

No one says anything about Pari, except for his stepmother, Parwana, who says that it had to be done in order to save the rest of the family. Abdullah feels Pari's absence, and digs up Pari's box of feathers. He vows that in the spring, he will leave and find her.

Character involvement:

- Abdullah narrates the chapter, and describes the family members. He insists on traveling with Father to Kabul.

- Father (Saboor) travels to Kabul and leaves Pari with a wealthy family.

- Uncle Nabi, Parwana's brother, arranges a construction job with his employers (the Wahdatis) in Kabul. Later, it is discovered he arranged for Pari to stay with his employers.

- Shuja, a large stray dog that follows Pari around, eventually leaves Shadbagh after Pari remains in Kabul.

Lessons learnt in this chapter: What KEY points did we learn?

- Pari, 3, and Abdullah, 10, are the children from Father's first marriage, and Abdullah essentially raised Pari from infancy after their mother died in childbirth.

- Pari collects feathers, and the sight of them reminds Abdullah of her. She is an innately happy person, like her mother was.

- Mrs. Wahdati visited their house in Shadbagh two years ago, and insisted on being treated equal to them all.

- Father's new wife, Parwana, is pregnant and has an infant son, Iqbal. Their first son, Omar, died at the age of only two weeks, during a bad winter.

-Father views the world as a harsh place, where nothing comes for free, and where the poor pay for things through suffering. Abdullah believes Father blames himself for Omar's death. Father is very reserved, except when he tells stories. Abdullah believes they are the truest part of Father.

What emotions are raised in this chapter?:

- After giving Pari away, Father is angry and withdrawn, and no longer tells stories.

- Parwana does not love Abdullah and Pari as much as Iqbal and Omar.

- Abdullah remembers how embarrassed they all were about their poverty when Mrs. Wahdati visited. He senses a feeling of something dangerous and broken in her at the bazaar.

- Abdullah fears being abandoned, and feels he no longer belongs with the family once Pari has gone.

-Father and Abdullah are very uncomfortable in the Wahdati home, and around the modern Mrs. Wahdati.

What questions are raised for the next chapter?:

- What will happen when Abdullah leaves in the spring to find Pari?

- Will Pari forget Abdullah as Qais forgot Baba Ayub in the fairytale?

- What will happen to Father now that he is sad he has lost Pari?

Chapter 3 - Chapter 3

Summary of chapter 3:

This chapter tells the story of Parwana's life and how she comes to marry Saboor. It alters between spring 1949 and her childhood. It begins with Parwana caring for her paralyzed twin sister, Masooma. Parwana has been the sole caregiver for her sister and has run the house since their parents' deaths. She catches sight of Saboor in town, who is said to be is looking for a new wife.

Then the story backtracks to Parwana's birth, where as babies, Masooma was well behaved and adored, while Parwana constantly cried and her relatives overlooked her. As age nine, Parwana developed a crush on Saboor. Saboor constantly told stories and said he wished to write his stories someday. One of his stories was that the giant oak tree that held the swing could grant wishes, and would shed ten leaves if it agreed to grant your wish. Parwana stole a notebook to give Saboor to write his stories, but was too scared to give it to Saboor.

When Masooma found it and gave it to Saboor, Parwana realized that they liked each other. Back to 1949, their brother Nabi visits, and says that Saboor mentioned he was looking for a new wife. Parwana thinks that Nabi is the person who best understands her, and knows of her feelings for Saboor. Back at age thirteen, Parwana saw how Masooma enjoyed her ability to attract men with her beauty, and felt horribly undesirable next to her sister. At age seventeen, while the twins were sitting high in the oak tree, Masooma revealed that Saboor would ask to marry her.

As she reached into her pocket to show how she knew it would happen, Parwana jostled the branch and lightly nudged her sister. The sisters both reached for each other as Masooma fell, but couldn't save her. Her back broke on the branch that held the swing, and as her family examined her on the ground, they found ten leaves in her hand. In 1949, Masooma requests Parwana to take her to Kabul. In the middle of the journey, Masooma asks Parwana to fill a hookah with a deadly amount of drugs, and then to leave her in the desert to die. Masooma bids Parwana to marry Saboor. After some argument, Parwana agrees and walks back home.

Character involvement: What each character is doing in this chapter.

- Parwana is Masooma's caregiver, and fulfills Masooma's request to help her to end her life. Parwana is about to begin her married life with Saboor.

- Masooma was always the preferred child, and as teenagers, Masooma was always admired for her beauty. Masooma and Saboor fell in love, and out of jealousy, Parwana caused Masooma to become paralyzed.

-Nabi works hard in Kabul and sends home money.

Lessons learnt in this chapter: What KEY points did we learn?

- Parwana was selfish when she put her love of Saboor over Masooma's life and happiness. Parwana shows her courage when she chooses to give her sister the death she desires, leaving Parwana to live with the guilt of doing so.
- Parwana thinks Saboor is a smaller version of himself since he wife died.

- Masooma wants to release both herself and Parwana from the burden of caring for her.

What emotions are raised in this chapter?:

- Parwana felt that life had given her sister beauty and denied it to herself. She felt crushed when she realized that Masooma and Saboor liked each other, and then again when she heard they would get married.

- Masooma and Parwana both feel trapped from Masooma's paralysis and need for constant care, but Parwana feels that she deserves the punishment.

-Nabi feels guilty for leaving because he cannot cope with the everyday care of Masooma.

- After Masooma's death, Parwana feels like she is being born into a new life.

What questions are raised for the next chapter?:

Is Parwana happy with her new life married to Saboor?

Does Saboor love Parwana as he loved Masooma?

Parwana says she will try to love Abdullah and Pari as her own—does something happen to change this?

Chapter 4 - Chapter 4

Summary of chapter 4:

This chapter tells Nabi's story as written in a letter from Nabi to Mr. Markos, when Nabi is near his death. Nabi first confesses that he left his home in Shadbagh because he felt it restricted his prospects. Nabi became a servant for Mr. Suleiman Wahdati, and would frequently drive and walk with him.

When Mr. Wahdati marries Nila, Nabi is overwhelmed by her beauty and individuality, and wishes to make her happy, as the Wahdati marriage is not a loving one. Nila has Nabi take her to see his family. On the journey home, she reveals that she cannot have children. Nabi wishes for her to love him, and comes up with the idea that she should adopt Pari as her daughter. And so Pari comes to live with them, and with time forgets Shadbagh. In 1955, Mr. Wahdati has a stroke, and becomes an invalid. Nila decides to move with Pari to Paris, France.

As Nila leaves, she tells Nabi that "it was always you," but Nabi doesn't understand what she means. Time passes, and Nabi finds Mr. Wahdati's old sketchbooks, and discovers all his drawings were of Nabi. In 1968, Mr. Wahdati confesses his love, in order to tell Nabi that he should leave him and start a family. Nabi realizes that he first stayed to care for Mr. Wahdati because of the guilt he felt for fleeing from caring for his sister, but remained because Mr. Wahdati was family, and provided a loving home. Mr. Wahdati makes Nabi promise something, since

Nabi refuses to leave. In 2000, Mr. Wahdati suffers another stroke, and shows Nabi his will, which leaves Nabi everything. He requests for Nabi to fulfill his promise, and Nabi eventually does, suffocating Suleiman with a pillow. In 2002, the Taliban had been driven out, and Mr. Markos knocks on the door.

Nabi offers for Mr. Markos free lodging, due to his aid work as a surgeon for Afghani children. Mr. Markos' friend Miss Amra finds an article that says Nila took her own life in 1974. In this letter, Nabi concludes by asking Mr. Markos to bury him near Mr. Wahdati, and to track down Pari. He asks Mr. Markos to give her this letter and his will, in which he leaves her everything, and to tell Pari that he hopes what he set in motion has led to happiness for her.

Character involvement: What each character is doing in this chapter.

- Nabi serves as Mr. Wahdati's servant and caregiver for most of his life.

- Suleiman Wahdati lives a solitary life, even in marriage, and loves Nabi from a distance. He leaves Nabi everything in his will.

- Nila Wahdati throws parties where she reads her sexual poems about lovers. She leaves with Pari to go to France after Mr. Wahdati's stroke.

-Cousins Idris and Timur Bashiri are young boys who play soccer in the street, and whose families leave Afghanistan in the 1980s.

- Mr. Markos stays at Nabi's house, and Nabi entrusts him to find Pari.

Lessons learnt in this chapter: What KEY points did we learn?

-Mr. Wahdati's life has been filled with the love he was able to have, and he desires to release Nabi from the restrictions of it.

-Nabi lived a life in service, in part to make up for abandoning the care of his sister.

-Nabi's life was full of love, and is empty without the companionship and care for Mr. Wahdati.

What emotions are raised in this chapter?:

- The unrequited romantic love of Mr. Wahdati for Nabi.

- Nabi's unrequited love for Nila, and his pride in bringing her happiness.

- Nabi feels resentful towards Pari for taking up all of Nila's attention.

- Saboor no longer wishes to see Nabi because Nabi broke up his family.

- The guilt of Nabi for tearing up a very pure love between children.

What questions are raised for the next chapter?:

What happened to Nabi and Nila in France?

What happens to Abdullah after Pari leaves for France? Are they reunited?

Is Mr. Markos able to find Pari?

Chapter 5 - Chapter 5

Summary of chapter 5:

This chapter begins in Spring 2003, when Idris and Timur return to visit Afghanistan. They go to a hospital to get a sense of the nation's tragedy, and meet the nurse Amra Ademovice. She shows them a girl named Rhosi whose skull was chopped open by an angry uncle, who murdered the rest of her family. Timur tells Amra that they have come to reconnect with their heritage and to understand what the country has gone through. Idris tells her later that they have come to reclaim their family's property to profit from renting to the international aid organizations.

They meet the surgeon Markos Varvaris, who invites them to a party at the house he is staying at. Idris thinks back to Timur's help when Idris's father died, about how Timur deliberately crafts his image as a generous person, advertising how he helps people. Idris and Timur reunite with Nabi at the house party.

Amra tells Idris that he is honest, and that Timur does not fool her. Amra tells Idris Rhosi's story. Idris buys Rhosi a TV, VCR, and tapes. He visits her and they form a bond, and he promises to fly her out to California so that she can get the surgery she needs. When Idris returns home to California, his family goes out for Afghan food at the restaurant owned by Abdullah, who gives them the meal for free, since Timur lent Abdullah the money to start the business.

Idris is remodeling his house and installing a home theatre.

He tells his wife Nahil that he wants to help people in Afghanistan, and she encourages him to do so, just like she sponsored a boy in Columbia. He goes to work, and is overwhelmed by all the work waiting for him. He eventually tells his boss about Roshi, and is relieved when she says the hospital will not be able to fund the surgery. His boss suggests that there are humanitarian groups that help, but he no longer wants the burden of fulfilling his commitment.

He adjusts back to his family life, convincing himself that he worked hard for and deserves his life. He tells himself that he overestimated his capabilities to help, and no longer responds to Amra's emails. Years later, Idris waits in a line for Roshi's book signing. The book is dedicated to Amra and Timur. Roshi writes in Idris's book not to worry, as she did not write about him.

Character involvement: What each character is doing in this chapter.

-Timur visits Afghanistan with his cousin Idris, and continues to visit to secure their Kabul family home. He helps Roshi get her surgery.

-Idris forms a bound with Roshi and promises to help her get her surgery, but then loses the drive to help once he returns home.

-Amra tells Idris Roshi's story, and emails him after he leaves to coordinate Roshi's operation.

- Abdullah and his wife, Sultana, own an Afghan restaurant in California. They married in Pakistan, and were granted asylum in the U.S. They have a daughter, Pari.

Lessons learnt in this chapter: What KEY points did we learn?

-Idris judges the expats harshly who visit Afghanistan in order to live through others' experiences and educate themselves on suffering.

-While Idris has good intentions and motivations, he is not brave enough to help Rhosi, but Timur is, even if it is for selfish reasons.

What emotions are raised in this chapter?:

- Idris resents the attitude of foreign visitors towards Afghani culture.

-Idris is jealous of Timur's ability to charm and get along with everyone.

-Idris resents his family's lack of appreciation and understanding of life in Afghanistan and their own privilege, but quickly readjusts.

What questions are raised for the next chapter?:

Will Idris and Timur find out their connection to

Abdullah?

What happened to Abdullah before he got to

Pakistan?

Chapter 6 - Chapter 6

Summary of chapter 6:

This chapter begins in February 1974, and tells of Pari's life in Paris. It begins with an excerpt from a magazine article, in which it announces Nila's death shortly after her interview was given for the magazine. The story moves to a short time before the interview, when Pari is called to the hospital to collect her mother. Pari is living with a professor who is much older than her, Julien, who formerly dated her mother. Nila has had a history of dramatics and alcoholism, and the doctor warns Pari about the harm Nila is causing herself.

In Nila's interview, she tells her history of life in Afghanistan, being restricted by a controlling father and culture. She claims she wished to save Pari from the same fate, but expresses in the interview her disappointment in Pari, even claiming that Pari is her punishment. Pari remembers how they met Julien when Pari was fourteen, in a hospital, and how he flirted with Nila, but truly desired Pari. Pari takes Nila home from the hospital, and straightens up Nila's apartment. Pari recalls how she met Julien at a protest her friend Colette organized, and moved in with Julien in part to escape living with Colette.

When Pari informs Nila she has moved in with Julien, Nila says that she doesn't really know who Pari is. Almost a year later, Julien forwards Pari the magazine article. Pari recalls Nila's funeral, and thinks on her doubts that she is Nila's biological daughter. Pari meets with Colette to discuss going to Afghanistan, but meets Colette's friend Eric. Pari and Eric marry, and plan to go to Afghanistan to trace Pari's biological family, but Pari becomes pregnant, so they postpone it. Pari no longer feels the need to go to Afghanistan because she has gained a sense of family and love with Eric and their three children. Eric dies after a series of heart attacks. In 2010, Pari receives a call from Markos, who reads the entire letter from Nabi over the phone. Pari's young memories flood back, and she fully remembers her brother. She decides to arrange a trip to Afghanistan.

Character involvement: What each character is doing in this chapter.

- Nila provides an interview for a magazine, shortly before committing suicide.

-Julien dates Nila when Pari is fourteen, but actually wishes to date Pari, and does so ten years later.

-Colette is friends with Pari, and becomes a student activist.

-Pari marries and has three children and a happy family life. She decides to go to Afghanistan after Markos calls Pari and reads Nabi's letter to her.

Lessons learnt in this chapter: What KEY points did we learn?

-Nila's poetry is an act of taking other people's stories and using them, and she says act of doing so is morally questionable.

-Nila married Mr. Wahdati after her operation, when she was disoriented with life and vulnerable.

- Pari feels that there is a hole in her life, which leads her to eventually believe she was adopted, and is missing a brother. She feels that she was supposed to serve a purpose to better Nila's life in some way, and that Nila's suicide meant she was not enough.

What emotions are raised in this chapter?:

-Pari enjoys math because it provides a constant, in contrast to life's ambiguities.

-Nila is dissatisfied with all of her relationships. Nila provides backhanded compliments to Pari, and hints that she is not beautiful.

-Pari feels guilt that her romance with Julien pushed Nila to suicide.

-Pari feels Julien's potential for cruelty, and compares it to Eric's decency.

What questions are raised for the next chapter?:

Will Pari return to Afghanistan?

Will Pari reunite with Abdullah?

Chapter 7 - Chapter 7

Summary of chapter 7:

This chapter takes place in Summer 2009, and introduces the character Adel, whose father razed Shadbagh and built a mansion house compound on the site. Adel's father, Commander Sahib, presides over the opening ceremony for the girls' school in New Shadbagh. The Commander disperses favors in the community, which he built up, through humanitarian work such as founding a free clinic and digging wells. An old man with spectacles and his son come forward to speak to the Commander, but Kabir, a guard, turns them away.

They return home, and Adel's father tells him that he must go away to tend to his responsibilities. He claims that the townspeople are dependent upon him, but that he would give his life for Adel. The old man and son come to the house and ask to see the Commander, but are turned away again. Kabir calls them buzzards to the Commander's generosity.

Adel sneaks out and meets the boy, Gholam. They play soccer and Gholam tricks Adel into giving him his prize soccer jersey. Gholam says that he has spent his whole life in a refugee camp in Pakistan with his father Iqbal and grandmother Parwana. They are now living in a tent on their old property to try to make a life there. When he next sees Gholam, he offers Adel his jersey back, saying he felt guilty about tricking Adel. Gholam reveals that the land Adel's father has built on actually belongs to them, and that they have the ownership documents to prove it.

Adel denies it and calls him a buzzard, and Gholam tells him that his father's factory in Helmand is growing something much worse than cotton. When Adel next sees Gholam, he offers him a winter coat as an act of kindness to counter Gholam's lies. But Gholam tells him that the judge, wearing a bribe of a shiny new watch, informed his father that the ownership documents were destroyed in a fire. Adel's father throws a party, and Iqbal throws stones at the house, breaking the windows. The Commander and his guards go outside and kill him.

Adel feels that he is turning into an adult, recognizing details he had not seen before: that his mother has secrets, that the townspeople are intimidated by and fear his father, and that he would likely accept this life because he had no other choice. He found a bloody pair of spectacles outside, and thinks he will feel relief at not having to think about the family again.

Character involvement: What each character is doing in this chapter.

- Adel meets Gholam, and learns that Iqbal owns the land Adel is living on.

- Iqbal attempts to get his land back, but the judge is bribed to burn his documents. Iqbal breaks the windows of the Commander's house, and the Commander kills him.

- Commander Sahib was a soldier in the jihad against the USSR invasion in the 1980s, and now directs the area of Shadbagh and owns what is implied to be heroin fields.

Lessons learnt in this chapter: What KEY points did we learn?

-Adel's father believes that a jihadist's sacrifice earns him special rights over others.

What emotions are raised in this chapter?:

- Adel admires his father, until he realizes that his father is not a good man, but corrupt.

-Adel is bored at his home, and is sad to have left Kabul and all of his friends.

-His mother is also bored, but has accepted her life.

What questions are raised for the next chapter?:

- Why did Abdullah stop sending the family money?

- Will Adel continue in his father's footsteps, or will this event change his choices?

- What will happen to Gholam and his family?

Chapter 8 - Chapter 8

Summary of chapter 8:

This chapter tells the story of Markos, as told from the first person. He begins in Fall 2010, listening to a voice message from his friend Thalia, who chastises him for not calling his mother. He thinks back to when he met Thalia in Summer 1967, when Thalia's mother, Madeleine, visited him and his mother, Odelia, on the island of Tinos, Greece. Odelia and Madeleine were childhood friends, and had promised to always stay close to each other, but hadn't seen each other in 15 years. Thalia was attacked by a dog when she was younger, and almost died from the botched surgery. Her face is disfigured, and her mother has her wear a mask to cover it.

As Markos calls Odelia, he mentions that Pari visited the house in Kabul, and Pari intended to visit Shadbagh and find Iqbal. Odelia urges him to come home soon, as she has just been diagnosed with Lou Gehrig's disease. Thinking back to Thalia's first visit, Markos was first horrified by Thalia's face, but grew to enjoy her company and not notice the disfigurement. Thalia created a homemade pinhole camera, and the first picture Markos takes is of Thalia. He carries this picture with him his entire life. Thalia's stepfather later left her an inheritance, and Thalia gave Markos half of it, for him to use to study. Markos traveled the world, waiting for inspiration to strike him for what to do, and winds up in an Indian hospital, where he volunteers to care for patients. Markos thinks back to when Madeleine left Thalia with them, and how Odelia helped the islanders accepted her as ordinary.

Thalia's stepfather offered to pay for Thalia to go to a private school in London, but Thalia chooses to stay with Odelia. Markos becomes a plastic surgeon to even the odds for people born without beauty. He receives a lot of money conducting cosmetic surgery in Athens, which allows him to spend much of his time volunteering to conduct surgery on children in developing countries. Amra calls Markos in 2002, saying her non-profit in Kabul is looking for a plastic surgeon for children. When Markos finally returns home, he learns that Odelia has begun following his news and work online. They watch a solar eclipse, and Markos feels that even with all of the time he has spent away, and how he and his mother do not get along, there is still good that can come from their relationship.

Character involvement: What each character is doing in this chapter.

- Markos leaves Tinos to escape his mother. He travels the world, and eventually works in Kabul.

-Madeleine leaves her daughter with her friend Odelia, and elopes with a film director.

-Odelia forms a strong bond with Thalia, and they live together on Tinos.

-Amra asks Markos to join her non-profit in Kabul.

- Thalia works as a handywoman/IT person, and refused an operation from Markos because she has accepted her face as a part of herself.

Lessons learnt in this chapter: What KEY points did we learn?

-Odelia's story of being left by first Madeleine and then Markos is echoed in Nila's abandonment of Mr. Wahdati.

-Odelia views kindness as creating indebtedness to the recipient, and resents when those she is kind to do not repay her to her satisfaction.

-Beauty is something a person has no control over, but it affects how the world views a person.

What emotions are raised in this chapter?:

-Markos thought he was a disappointment to his
mother, but finds out she is proud of him.

-Markos feels a hole in his life returning home, like
he has missed out on the story of Odelia's and
Thalia's lives.

-Markos feels that his mother was lonely and needy,
but he is grateful that she gave him the gift of
security, that she would never abandon him.

What questions are raised for the next chapter?:

- Does Pari find Iqbal?

- Does Pari reconnect with Abdullah?

Chapter 9 - Chapter 9

Summary of chapter 9:

This chapter tells the story of Abdullah's daughter,
Pari, as told from the first person. It begins in Winter
2010. Pari tells of how when she was younger,
Abdullah would tell her wonderful bedtime stories,
including about his sister, Pari. Pari would pretend
that her Aunt Pari was actually her invisible sister.

Pari dreamed that she would save up money and
travel to buy her Aunt Pari back for her father. Pari
picks up her Aunt Pari from the airport, and they
begin to talk about their families. Pari thinks back to
when she was a child, and could not engage in many
of the school activities because of her religion and

culture. Pari went to Farsi lessons and Koran lessons and helped at the restaurant. She accepted a scholarship for an art school in Baltimore, but then her mother is found to have a tumor. Before her mother dies, she tells Pari that Abdullah is sending money to their family in Afghanistan. Aunt Pari meets Abdullah, but he does not recognize her due to his dementia.

Aunt Pari shows Pari her pictures from Afghanistan, and tells her that she thinks something happened to Iqbal. Aunt Pari also shows her pictures of her family, and tells her how Nila always had holes that Aunt Pari was expected to fill. Aunt Pari stays for a month, and Abdullah gets very angry when Aunt Pari says she is his sister. Pari shows Aunt Pari the letters she wrote to her when she was little. Later, Abdullah has a stroke and Pari moves him into an assisted-living home.

Pari finds a package in the house from Abdullah for Aunt Pari. When Pari visits Aunt Pari in France, she hands her the package. It is Aunt Pari's feather box, and while she cannot remember it, she appreciates the sentiment. Pari is excited to meet her family. As Aunt Pari sleeps, Pari thinks of the game she used to play with Abdullah, giving him a dream that he was with his sister, and does the same for Aunt Pari.

Character involvement: What each character is doing in this chapter.

- Pari gives up a scholarship to art college in order to care for first her mother, then her father.

- Aunt Pari comes to meet Abdullah, and has Pari come visit her family in France.

- Abdullah is suffering from dementia.

Lessons learnt in this chapter: What KEY points did we learn?

- Aunt Pari feels like because she doesn't know where she came from, she is in the middle of a story, trying to figure out the beginning.

- Abdullah has trapped Pari into her life with his love and fear of abandonment.

- Pari always felt a presence with her, and Aunt Pari always felt an absence. They were both missing their incomplete part of their family.

What emotions are raised in this chapter?:

- Pari knows that others admire her for her sacrifice for her parents, but she sometimes feels resentful for making the sacrifice.

- Pari is afraid of being free because she is so used to her life now.

- Pari feels Abdullah's love forced her into a choice of either having to fight to be smothered from it, or fleeing it completely.

- Aunt Pari is happy to have found Abdullah, even if he is not present.

- Pari and Aunt Pari are happy to have found each other.

What questions remain unanswered?:

What has happened to Iqbal's family?

What happened to Abdullah after his sister Pari was taken away?

OVERALL Book Summary:

The book begins on the eve of Father's journey. He tells his children a bedtime story about a man who gives up the child he loves so that the rest of the family may survive, and so that the child might have a better opportunity. The next day, Father, Abdullah, and Pari travel to Kabul, Father pulling Pari in a wagon. They meet the wealthy Suleimon and Nila Wahdati, who employ the children's step-uncle. Nila adopts Pari, separating the two siblings.

Then, we learn the story of Parwana, their stepmother, who was in love with their father, Saboor, even as a child. Parwana suffered over her lack of beauty compared to her sister. Her sister was supposed to marry Saboor, but upon hearing the news, Parwana caused her sister to fall out of a tree

and break her spine. Parwana cares for her sister, until
she requests that Parwana help her to commit suicide.
She bids Parwana to marry Saboor, whose first wife
died.

We next learn the step-uncle Nabi's story, through a
letter he wrote to Markos. He went to work for Mr.
Wahdati, and was enthralled by Nila's beauty. He
wished to make Nila happy, and since Nila could not
have children, he suggested she adopt Pari. After Mr.
Wahdati's stroke, Nila leaves, taking Pari with her to
Paris. Nabi cares for Mr. Wahdati up through the
Taliban rule, continuing even after discovering Mr.
Wahdati is in love with him. Nabi also assists Mr.
Wahdati in committing suicide, and Mr. Wahdati
leaves everything to Nabi in his will. After the
American military removes the Taliban from power,

Mr. Wahdati lets Markos, a plastic surgeon with the humanitarian groups, stay at the house for free.

Idris and Timur, who had lived on the same street as Mr. Wahdati and Nabi, return to Kabul after years in America in order to reclaim their family's house. Markos invites them to a party where they see Nabi again. Idris, a doctor, meets a girl, Roshi, in desperate need for surgery. He promises to get her the surgery, but after returning home, abandons the idea. Years later, Roshi has published a book about her life, and Idris goes to her book signing to apologize to her.

He finds that Timur helped her to get the surgery. Then we move to Pari's life in France with Nila, who has become an alcoholic. Nila gives an interview shortly before her suicide, in which she tells her difficulties as a rebellious young woman in Afghanistan, and expresses her disappointment in Pari. Pari began an affair with a man Nila had previously dated, and believes that is what drove Nila to the breaking point. Pari marries Eric, a kind man, and has a happy family life. A few years after her husband's death, Markos calls her, reads aloud Nabi's letter, and Pari decides to visit Afghanistan. Then the story moves to Markos, describing his childhood on the island of Timos, Greece. His childhood friend, Thalia, was abandoned by her mother, Madeleine, who was his mother's childhood friend.

Thalia has a disfiguring scar from a dog attack and botched surgery, and provides some of her inheritance money for Markos to go to university. She never leaves the island, happy with her acceptance there.

Markos travels the world, eventually inspired to become a plastic surgeon. He earns money from his practice in order to finance his volunteering to operate on children in developing countries, helping them to overcome the luck they have been cast in the genetic lottery.

He goes to Kabul temporarily, but ends up staying for years. He returns home to visit and reconnects with his mother. Finally, we move to Abdullah, as told through the eyes of his daughter, Pari. Abdullah received political asylum with his wife, and moved to California, where Pari was born. Pari gave up her scholarship at an art school in order to care first for her mother during her illness, and then for her father, who is suffering from dementia. The older Aunt Pari tracks them down, and comes to visit. While

Abdullah does not recognize her, she is happy just to be in her brother's presence. Both the niece and aunt are happy to be connected and to fill part of their lives with a missing piece.

Thank you!

We hope you enjoyed our chapter by chapter review

EasyToDigest

Made in United States
North Haven, CT
31 May 2023

37204575R00039